THE GOAL TENDER

A JOURNEY TO LIVING THE LIFE OF YOUR DREAMS

SHAWN DOYLE CSP

© Copyright 2018–Shawn Doyle

All rights reserved. This book is protected by the copyright laws of the United States of America. This book may not be copied or reprinted for commercial gain or profit. The use of short quotations or occasional page copying for personal or group study is permitted and encouraged. Permission will be granted upon request. For permissions requests, write to the publisher, addressed "Attention: Permissions Coordinator," at the address below.

SOUND WISDOM
P.O. Box 310
Shippensburg, PA 17257-0310

For more information on publishing and distribution rights, call 717-530-2122 or info@soundwisdom.com.

Quantity Sales. Special discounts are available on quantity purchases by corporations, associations, and others. For details, contact the Sales Department at Sound Wisdom.

While efforts have been made to verify information contained in this publication, neither the author nor the publisher assumes any responsibility for errors, inaccuracies, or omissions.

While this publication is chock-full of useful, practical information, it is not intended to be legal or accounting advice. All readers are advised to seek competent lawyers and accountants to follow laws and regulations that may apply to specific situations.

The reader of this publication assumes responsibility for the use of the information. The author and publisher assume no responsibility or liability whatsoever on the behalf of the reader of this publication.

ISBN 13 TP: 978-1-937879-98-3
ISBN 13 Ebook: 978-1-937879-99-0

For Worldwide Distribution, Printed in the U.S.A.
1 2 3 4 5 6 7 8 / 21 20 19 18

Cover/Jacket designer Eileen Rockwell
Interior design by Susan Ramundo

DEDICATION

I have been given such a great gift in my life. A miracle that never ever stops amazing me—my beautiful wife Rachael.

Thank you for motivating and inspiring me every day. You are amazing.

CONTENTS

Chapter One	9
Chapter Two	23
Chapter Three	33
Chapter Four	43
Chapter Five	57
Chapter Six	69
Chapter Seven	83
Chapter Eight	93
Chapter Nine	105
Chapter Ten	117
Action Planner	131

CHAPTER ONE

It doesn't matter whether someone thinks I'm short or tall, but it matters if I stand tall in my own eyes—because I know my disciplines, I know what I'm doing, I know whether I'm doing it or not doing it. It doesn't have to be published in some local paper, as long as I know that I'm paying the price and that I deserve the applause and I deserve the prize. That's what's exciting. That's why this goal setting is so important. It challenges you to grow. It challenges you to become more than you are, to move up to the next level. And that's key.

—JIM ROHN

Joe Gregory stood on the train platform in his tan overcoat. It was a grey, chilly watercolor of a fall morning. The relentless cold rain kept insulting him by blowing down the collar of his coat, and he could feel it running down the back of his neck. He hated Monday. It just reminded him of how much he hated this job of his. He shifted and pulled his collar together more tightly and sighed. He muttered "C'mon stupid train!" between his teeth to no one in particular as he looked at his watch again. The Monday morning commute was always the worst. The beginning of yet another week that Joe was not excited about. Drive twenty minutes to the train, get everything out of the car, insert coins in the numbered metal slot of the parking coin box, and ride the train an hour into the city. Work, work, work, work. Reverse the whole routine on the way home if everything was on time. He sighed and tried to remember a time when he was excited to go to work. When was that? Boy, it was a long time ago. The rumbling of the train followed by the braking sounds snapped Joe out of his thoughts and into the routine of scrambling for a choice window seat.

He settled into his seat and looked around at all the familiar faces that were always on the 6:07 A.M. train. He knew all the faces, but ironically, after riding this same train the same time every weekday for five years, he didn't know one name. *Surely*, he thought to himself, *I must know someone's name?* He was embarrassed to admit he didn't know any. After all, no one talked on trains—it was kind of an unspoken rule. He recognized the sock lady, the one who always wore the crazy socks—even with a dress; the teen with the prep school blazer and tie who looked like a Ralph Lauren ad; the man with jeans and sloppy tee shirts who looked like a computer programmer; and Mr. Umbrella, who always had a fancy wooden umbrella even on sunny days, just in case it rained. He didn't know them and would admit, if pressed, that he didn't really want to. This commute every day was too draining to have to feel obligated to talk to your train

CHAPTER ONE

buddy to and from work. The reality is they didn't want to talk either. They were *The Commuters*, a silent army of heroes who understood the task—to just shut up and get to work. No idle chitchat needed or asked for! No, they knew the task and didn't mess around about it. Let's be serious and get to work!

"Good morning."

Joe looked up from his seat and saw a slim man, elegantly dressed in a suit, standing there. He was holding a paper cup of coffee and had a *Wall Street Journal* folded under his arm.

"Oh, Uh…good morning," Joe said.

The gentleman smiled and said, "OK if I sit here?"

Joe looked up and said, "Yeah, have a seat." He looked away and didn't make eye contact. He realized afterward that he didn't sound very nice about it and wished he had said it a little more cheerfully.

The older gentleman sat down and tapped Joe on the shoulder and smiled.

The man stuck out his hand toward Joe and said, "I am Michael—it's nice to meet you, and you are…?"

THE GOAL TENDER

"Joe Gregory—nice to meet you too."

Didn't this man know the rules? For gosh sakes, he was trying to have some peace.

The train pulled away from the stop. The conductor loudly barked out "Next Stop: Paolilloiiii…," and no one except the veteran riders understood a word the conductor just said. New train riders were looking at their train schedules and trying to figure out what was just announced.

The gentleman smiled at Joe. "So…it's a beautiful morning, isn't it?"

Joe gave him a sarcastic look and frowned. "You're kidding me, right?"

Michael smiled a broad smile and said, "Oh no, I am being sincere. I think a rainy morning can be quite…beautiful, in fact. Kind of like one of those cool movies from the old days. So how is your morning going?"

Joe kind of wondered where this guy was from and why he was lucky enough that "Mr. Positive" decided to sit next to him that morning. Joe sighed and said, "Well, you know—living the dream."

CHAPTER ONE

Michael chuckled quietly.

Joe gave Michael a puzzled look. "Something tickle your funny bone there, Michael?"

Michael looked over at Joe. "Oh, no. OK well, sort of, I guess." Michael shrugged. "I just think it is kind of humorous that when people say living the dream, that is almost always the opposite of what they really mean. It's always an ironic statement they are making, as indicated by their tone." He smiled warmly.

"Well, to be honest, it's Monday, I hate the rain, my job sucks, and every day I ride this blasted train into the city, and it's just a grind. It's sucking out my soul. So there is a report on my day so far. How does that sound?" Joe immediately regretted pouring out his heart to some guy that just sat down next to him on the train. *Why am I being so mean? Why am I doing this? What is wrong with me?* He thought. *Does this guy Michael have some sort of magic power to make me confess my thoughts?*

Michael looked over at Joe. "I understand," he said in a very warm way, without judgment or criticism.

Joe was a little surprised and said, "You do? You understand?"

THE GOAL TENDER

Michael looked around the train. He leaned toward Joe and said in a low, conspiratorial tone, "Sure. I would say most people on this train feel the same way. They don't love their jobs, and they too are living for the weekend." He smiled.

"Just like you?" Joe said.

Michael sat back and smiled. "Oh no, my heavens, not me. No. I am kind of retired. I go in to work when I want. I love my life."

Joe said, "Man…that sounds nice."

Michael thoughtfully took a sip from his coffee. "So Joe, can I ask you a question? I mean, you don't have to answer if you don't want to."

"OK—shoot."

Michael said, "What would you love to do for work? What are you really passionate about? That is, if you could choose."

Joe said, "But that answer doesn't matter—why think about what I can't have?"

"Well, Joe, I think that you are the architect of your own life. You can decide to do anything you want."

CHAPTER ONE

"OK, I will play your little game to humor you. As weird as this sounds, I have a passion for baking. There…I said it out loud. Cakes, pies, cookies, you name it. I love baking, and people at work go crazy over my stuff when I bring in my baked goods. So what do you think about that?"

"I think it can be a very good business. Who doesn't love a fresh-baked cookie?"

Joe looked at Michael. "So, Michael, I am going to just quit my lousy job and open up a bakery on Main Street tomorrow and live happily ever after? Everything is just going to be sunshine and unicorns? Is that what you are saying?"

Michael looked at Joe and shook his head. "No, that is not exactly what I am saying. I am saying that it can be a long-term goal you work toward."

Joe waved a dismissive hand at Michael. "Right…like that would ever happen."

"Well, I believe you *can make it* happen."

Joe said, "Well, how can I make it happen? I have bills, I work tons of hours every week, I don't have money to finance a business, I have a mortgage. Do you have a magic wand I can borrow?"

Michael chuckled. "No, I am afraid not. I forgot to pack it in my briefcase today. But I do have a system you can use to make sure you probably aren't riding this train three years from now."

"Really, like what?"

"Goal setting," Michael said with confidence.

"Goal setting? Like that would work?"

Michael held up his hand. "Wait, hear me out. Have you ever heard of Famous Amos, the chocolate chip cookie guy? Or Ann Bealer, the founder of Auntie Anne's Pretzels? Have you heard of Mrs. Fields, another great example of someone who did well in baked products?"

Joe said, "Yeah, I have heard of a few of them, but I bet they were born with silver spoons in their mouths or had some Sugar Daddy or Sugar Momma to start them out."

Michael shook his head and took a thoughtful sip of his coffee. "No Joe, I think you will find the exact opposite—they all had almost nothing but, through the power of goal setting, made their dreams come true."

CHAPTER ONE

Joe smirked and said, "You know, I like how you use the word *made*. Like they just snapped their fingers and made it happen."

Michael put up a patient hand in response. "I know what you are saying, young man. But here is something to really think about—it all begins here, in your mind." Michael pointed at his head. "I have read and studied about this many times—you are what you think about, and yes, you can reinvent your life if you make a serious attempt at setting goals, putting them in writing, and following a system."

Joe sat back in his seat. "Well, you know, that is kind of interesting. Back in the day, when I was in high school, I was involved in a lot of things, and I was sure I was going to grow up and have my own business. I remember thinking that. I was passionate about that. Then when I graduated college, well…I don't know—life just kind of ran away from me." He sighed. "I forgot the dream in all the busy aspects of life."

"The good news is it's not too late to change everything. Just like someone would tend to a garden, you must tend to your life so that your life grows and blossoms. The most important way is to have goals. You must have goals and be a **Goal Tender**. This is a gift I am giving you this morning that you must not underestimate because it can change your whole life!" Michael had a spark in his eye.

Joe was struck by how Michael said that with such passion in his voice. Joe said, "I admit you have some good points. So… where the heck would I start? I don't know how to begin."

Michael said, "That is a good question. Sometime this week, maybe during all your train time, take out a piece of paper, and write down your goals. As Tony Robbins once said, 'Setting goals is the first step in turning the invisible into the visible.'"

"Hmmm…that is pretty simple. That is something I could do this week."

Michael said, "Excellent! That is the spirit. You see, once you start doing that, you will also get excited. You will no longer be stagnant. Your life will be moving in the right direction. You will reignite your enthusiasm, wake up your passion, and feel more hopeful."

"I just feel kind of silly—in my whole life I have never written down my goals before. I mean, I knew about it; I just didn't do it," Joe said with a tone of regret, shaking his head.

Michael held up his hand, and he had three fingers up. "Well, you are not alone. Research based on a Harvard study indicates that, shockingly, only three percent of the population has clearly articulated goals. Isn't that amazing? That

CHAPTER ONE

means that 97 percent of the people on this train, going to work, don't know why they are doing it. So which are you? The top three percent or the rest of the sheep going to the slaughter?" Michael chuckled.

Joe said, "Well, what do you think?"

"I just met you, but I think that you are very smart and have unlimited potential! I think you have a fire inside of you—I see it. Also remember this—the people that don't have goals often end *working* for those who do! You have to think about this, and in your train time this week, make it happen. Write out your goals to start moving forward. It will feel great."

Joe said, "I am going to. Wow. Thanks for the great tips and ideas. What do I owe you?"

Michael smiled and said, "For what?"

Joe smiled back and said, "For the motivational seminar."

"Oh, nothing at all. I love sharing the stuff that has really helped me. Why don't you give me your card, and I will send you an email later this week."

Joe handed Michael a card. "Yes, that would be great."

THE GOAL TENDER

The conductor came down the aisle, yelling loudly enough to wake the dead and the people who had nodded off during their commute, "NEXT STOP CCEEENNNETTTERR CITYEEEEE…"

The train started slowing down.

Michael looked over at Joe and said, "Well, this is my stop. I really enjoyed talking with you. Have a great day!"

"You too," Joe said. "It also looks like it stopped raining."

Right after lunch, Joe received an email from Michael:

> Dear Joe,
>
> It was a real pleasure meeting you today and talking with you. I think you are extremely bright and you have unlimited potential! I enjoyed talking with you so much that my coffee got cold. (I forgive you.)
>
> I am glad you think it is a good idea to write down your goals.
>
> You may also want to think about **buying a journal** to start writing your goals in, to track their progress,

CHAPTER ONE

and to record your thoughts. I have found this to be very helpful in my life.

Here are a few quotes I thought you would enjoy about goals:

"You control your future, your destiny. What you think about comes about. By recording your dreams and goals on paper, you set in motion the process of becoming the person you most want to be. Put your future in good hands—your own."—*Mark Victor Hansen*

"The new year stands before us, like a chapter in a book, waiting to be written. We can help write that story by setting goals."—*Melody Beattie*

So I hope you find this information and these ideas helpful and inspiring.

If you want to talk again sometime on the train, I always take the 6:07 when I go in to the city and always ride in car #4. Would love to catch up and see how you are doing. I usually go into the city on Wednesdays and Fridays. Look for me if you would like to talk again.

THE GOAL TENDER

By the way I am looking forward to walking into one of your bakeries in the future and buying one of my favorite cookies, oatmeal raisin. (I might just splurge and buy two.)

Make it a great day.

Your new friend,

Michael

CHAPTER TWO

When people say, "You're not being realistic," they're just trying to tag some thoughts that they can't otherwise handle.

—DAVID R. BROWER

Two weeks later, Joe was in car #4 and was looking out the window, thinking about his goals. In last two weeks, the trees had started producing their beautiful, autumn colors. The speed of the train melted them into a candy-corn-infused blur as the train rolled on down the tracks. Joe was reflecting on how much his thinking had changed in the last two weeks. It was as if a door in his mind had opened that was previously locked tight, or maybe he didn't know there was a door at all before. He wasn't sure; he just knew things were different and his mindset was changing.

"Well, look who is sitting on my train again."

Joe looked over and saw Michael standing there.

"Michael—wow! How are you? Please have a seat!" Joe was beaming at Michael.

"Thanks."

Michael sat down and smiled over at Joe. "I am doing well. How are you doing?"

Joe nodded and said, "Well…I am actually doing great. It is really wonderful to see you. I have a lot to share with you, if you would like to hear about it."

"Oh good," Michael said. "So tell me what is going on in your life? Did you get my email?"

Joe said, "Yes, I sure did—that was very kind of you. It was super helpful. In fact, I took one of your suggestions." He reached into his briefcase and rummaged around. He proudly held up a small, red, hardbound book. "I bought a journal and have been writing down my goals!"

Michael took a sip of his coffee and said, "Well, that is wonderful news! You are quite the student, Joe. Many people take advice but don't take action, but you do. Good for you. How has writing out your goals worked so far?"

CHAPTER TWO

"Well, it has gone well—I have written out my goals. It was a good feeling to get them down on paper. I feel like this is the first big step, and I have done it."

Michael smiled. "If you don't mind too much, and if it's not too personal, would you share a few of them with me?"

"Of course!" Joe said. "I mean—our discussion a few weeks ago really got me thinking." He opened the book to the first page. "1) To set up a website and starting selling my Joe and Jimmy's cookies online by June of next year. 2) To generate $3,500 in sales by the end of the fourth quarter."

"So that is pretty impressive. You already have a product name and a goal that has a timetable and measurement for success… very nice job. I just have one question—who is this Jimmy person?" Michael smiled. "I didn't know you had a partner."

Joe sat back in his seat, smiling. "Well, I have this idea for the brand: it's me and Jimmy, who is not a person but my dog. He is the cutest little pug, and people love dogs! I have this buddy of mine who is a great cartoonist, and he is going to design a logo for me."

"Very good, young man, and I am impressed with what you have done so far. I really like the name and the brand idea. Very creative approach. The name has a nice ring to it. "

THE GOAL TENDER

"Thanks," Joe said.

"Have you found this first step of the goal tending process challenging?"

Joe nodded slowly as Michael was talking. "Yeah, now that you mention it, there is just one thing I am wrestling with a little right now."

"OK," Michael said. "I must be honest: I see one issue. But let's start with the one you see first."

"Well…I guess I struggle a little bit with whether this goal is *realistic* or not. I don't know…I am not a famous chef or some celebrity—why would people buy cookies from me? I am not sure I believe it is possible."

Michael chuckled. "Yes, I understand. But why not you? If your cookies are great, then that is all that matters. You don't have to be famous, but you could be in the future."

"I guess so, but…do you think it is realistic?" Joe asked.

Michael raised his index finger to make a point. "It really doesn't matter what I think. But here is a more important point—what does realistic mean? It is something you have to watch out for with people who want to define realistic

CHAPTER TWO

for you. A few years ago electric cars were not realistic. But someone believed they were realistic—or maybe another way of saying it, they were *possible*. People said Amazon, Tesla, Apple iTunes, and Uber were not realistic and, in fact, would never gain acceptance in our society. All of the people that created those things moved forward *despite* the naysayers telling them it wasn't realistic. Realistic is a very subjective term that is dependent on the perception of each person, and those people may be dead wrong. It is a word I have never liked all my life and you know why?"

Joe paused and said, "No…why?"

"Because the word *realistic* is a verbal weapon used by negative people to create limitations and influence others to limit their thinking. We are riding on a nice train today that was at some point not realistic until someone had a vision and built a locomotive. I would remove that ridiculous word from your vocabulary and thinking completely."

"Good point. To give you a real example, my brother-in-law said my business idea was ridiculous."

Michael shook his head and sighed. He paused for a moment. "I am not criticizing your brother-in-law, but there are always naysayers. They always delight in tearing people down and demeaning their ideas. Mark my words—the biggest mistake you can make is listening to those toxic, negative people. I read this book one time called *Jumpstart Your Motivation*, and the author mentions ESVs, which he defined as 'Energy Sucking Vampires.' These people do exist, you know, and there are far too many of them. As Sophocles once said, 'No enemy is worse than bad advice.' You just need to ignore them and move forward."

"Yes, you know what? You are so right," said Joe, nodding his head, deep in thought.

"I have never cared for the SMART goal formula, which I'm sure you have heard about. It stands for Specific, Measurable, Achievable, Realistic, and Timely. The words *achievable* and *realistic* in that formula always stuck in my craw."

Joe nodded. "Because achievable is another limiting word."

"Yes! Now you are catching on, my young friend. Very good. I think goals should be SMT: Specific, Measurable, and Timely. Forget the ridiculous limiting words like *realistic* and *achievable*."

"Got it."

Michael paused briefly. "So, may I ask you a question?"

CHAPTER TWO

"Sure—anything," said Joe.

"How will you, Joe, work on changing your belief about what is realistic?"

"Well," Joe said. "I am not so sure that I can. They are beliefs I have always had my whole life—right?"

Michael took a thoughtful sip of coffee. "The question to ask yourself is this—really, what are beliefs? They are merely a collection of ideas you have about something based your upbringing, your experiences, and your studies. It doesn't mean they are true, just that you adopted them. The worst part is, until now, you never questioned them."

"That makes sense," said Joe.

Michael said with a spark in his eye, "So, if a belief is a collection of ideas about something, then we can change our ideas, which will change our belief! We have that power!"

"I have never thought of it that way before. So how do I change the ideas that make up the belief?" asked Joe.

Michael said, "Good question, sir. There are several ways: 1) A mentor or coach can get you to think differently; 2) Reading about other people who have done what you want to do can help change your beliefs, because someone else has already done it; 3) You can take online or live training; and 4) You can write down your beliefs in your journal so that you can see them, evaluate them, and then change them."

Joe said, "Super! Those are great ideas. Thanks so much."

Michael said, "The pleasure is all mine. In my mind, the missing aspect of goal setting is *how people think* about goals. You are fun to talk to, Joe, because you are so open to learning."

The train started slowing down as it pulled into the station.

Michael said, "Oh, here is my stop—I would love to talk again some time."

"I guarantee we will. Same train, same seat—different morning."

"So long for now, Michael," said Joe.

Michael smiled and nodded.

Later that day, Joe received another thoughtful email from Michael:

CHAPTER TWO

Dear Joe,

What a delightful conversation today with you yet again. I must say I really enjoy talking with you, and I am very thrilled with your progress. I enjoyed it so much that I didn't even look at my paper once on the train. So now my *Wall Street Journal* reading backlog is your fault!

I can see a day in the near future when I will go online and order some of those cookies from Joe and Jimmy's. I really like the name.

Remember to constantly be **vigilant about your thinking** and to challenge what you think is **realistic** (and possible). Your beliefs can hold you back, but they can be changed.

Here are few quotes I thought you might really enjoy and find valuable:

"Your time is limited, so don't waste it living someone else's life. Don't be trapped by dogma—which is living with the results of other people's thinking. Don't let the noise of others' opinions drown out your own inner voice. And most important, have the courage to follow your heart and intuition."—*Steve Jobs*

THE GOAL TENDER

"I believe we create our own lives. And we create it by our thinking, feeling patterns in our belief system. I think we're all born with this huge canvas in front of us and the paintbrushes and the paint, and we choose what to put on this canvas." —*Louise Hay*

So I hope you find these ideas helpful and inspiring.

Your Friend,

Michael

CHAPTER THREE

Stay focused, go after your dreams and keep moving toward your goals.

—LL COOL J

Two weeks later, Joe was back on his morning train, heading into the city. He had pulled out his book, and he was reading through his goals and reviewing the progress he had made. He smiled and sighed and felt good that he had made so much progress. Joe wondered at the same time why he had not done this sooner—like about five years before. What was he waiting for? He didn't like the fact that he had wasted so many years. He felt in some ways that he had been in a fog, just kind of going through the motions. Why had it taken him so long to wake up? He wasn't going to dwell too much on the past because all that mattered now was he was on the right track. He smiled at the pun he had created for himself, thinking about being in the right track while riding on the train. He realized that his whole demeanor was changing and he was having more of a sense of humor about himself. The "old him" was coming back, the one who was excited, upbeat, and optimistic.

"Looks like you are deep in thought, my young friend."

Joe looked up and saw Michael standing there, resplendent in his long black coat, grey suit, and red tie. Joe smiled broadly.

"May I join you?" Michael asked, motioning to the seat.

"Oh my, of course, yes, by all means—please have a seat."

Michael settled into his seat and glanced over at Joe. "So super student—how are we doing?"

"I am doing great! It is so great to see you again. I have a lot to share with you. I have done some work and have made some good progress. I am very excited."

Michael nodded and raised a quizzical eyebrow. "What would you like to share?"

Joe opened up his book. "Well, first of all, I have hired my friend to design the logo for my company. He has already given me some rough sketches. They look really good so far."

Michael nodded. "That is very good news. So let me ask you a question. How does it feel seeing a rough design of your new company logo?"

CHAPTER THREE

Joe said, "It is really exciting! It sounds kind of silly, but I get excited just seeing it. It seems...well, it just makes it so much more real. Like really real!" Joe's eyes lit up when he said it.

Michael chuckled. "Yes, you are very right. It makes it more tangible. I was just doing my daily morning reading and came across a quote that I wrote down." Michael pulled out a small, brown, leather, pocket-size journal. "Ah, here it is—it's a quote by Robert Collier: 'Visualize this thing that you want, see it, feel it, believe in it. Make your mental blueprint, and begin to build.'

"Yes, that is exactly it—my blueprint is helping. I am starting to visualize it, like I would if I were building a house with a blueprint."

Michael said, "If you are going to build this business, and I believe you will, you will have to do a lot of work, and some of the work is going to be in your mind. You have to change your mindset from that of an employee to one of an owner. You have to expand your thinking and think much bigger."

"Yes, I agree. This whole process has already helped me start to think differently and, I guess, bigger too. I took your advice, and I have been reading a book about Anne Beiler, the founder of Auntie Anne's pretzels. I picked that one because she is from this local area. It is a really interesting story. She only has a ninth-grade education and started out selling at a small stand not too far from where I live."

Michael nodded. "Yes, I have had her products a few times in airports—quite tasty, I might add. I know a little bit about her story. I believe that I recently saw an article which mentioned that the company just sold for millions to an investment firm. So what did you get out of reading about her and her business?"

Joe said, "I guess I found it to be very inspirational. I was amazed by what she did. As I was reading it, I thought to myself—if she can do it, then why can't I? Yes, that is right, why not me? I mean, I have a degree in marketing, lots of business experience, and a college education. I realized that I can achieve her level of success, but I have to be careful about my mindset."

"That is the spirit. Why not you?" said Michael, pointing at Joe. "Here is what I think...I think you are very bright and have the two other important qualities: you have passion and a great product. You can be the next Auntie Anne's. Why not you, Joe? Why not Joe and Jimmy's?"

"I also hired a very gifted designer who is going to create my website after the logo is done. I am pleased that I can cross

CHAPTER THREE

this off my list as well. So I am on track to start selling by June of this year."

"Excellent." Michael smiled. "When you are a multimillionaire, will you pretend like you still know me when you see me on the train?"

Joe waived his hand dismissively. "Of course I will, Michael! But my dream is to work out of my home office, so I won't be riding the train into the city anymore, which I won't miss—except for talking to you, of course."

"Well said." Michael nodded.

"That is where I am right now, Michael. So what do you think are the next steps in my process?"

"Good question," Michael said. "I think now you need to work on some blue-sky, big thinking and draft a few very important documents. What I mean by that is here is where you need to start thinking expansively. This is a very important part of the process, in my opinion. You need to create a mission and vision statement."

"Hmm," said Joe. "I have a question about that. With all due respect—why do I need that if I already have my timeline and my initial sales goal?"

THE GOAL TENDER

"Good question. That was just your initial goal to start getting you excited about the possibilities. The biggest mistake I see is that people set goals without thinking about and articulating *the why behind them*. You want to start a cookie company. Why?"

"To leave a job I don't enjoy," Joe blurted out.

"OK, that is fair. But is the mission of your new company going to be 'Buy a cookie so Joe can leave his job?' With all due respect, I don't think so. The why it has to be something bigger, something people can embrace. Steve Jobs wanted to make a ding in the universe. Martin Luther King Jr. wanted to change the way people thought about race and equality."

"Well, that makes sense, but—to be the devil's advocate here for a moment—I am not starting a high-tech product company or a civil rights movement. It's just about cookies, right?"

Michael held up a finger. "Yes, but what if it wasn't? For example, Tom's Shoes gives away a pair of shoes to someone in need every time a person buys a pair of their shoes. So then they have a mission. I am making this up, but what if your mission was to bring a tiny bit of joy to people each day in the form of a cookie? In a troubled world, I can have just a moment of joy. What if you had a foundation to fund

CHAPTER THREE

other people who wanted to start a business and quit the job they hated, and you called it the Cookie Jar Fund? I am just throwing that out there, but you know what I mean. Now you have a mission. A mission is something beyond the money. To be clear, you need the money because that is the purpose of a company—to generate capital—but you also need a mission. Something bigger than the money, something that can change the world."

Joe whistled lowly. "I see what you are saying now—all I can say is wow! It's like a smack in my head! I don't know why I didn't think of that. I can also see that as we hire people, we can choose employees who believe what we believe and support our company's mission. We can also tell our customers the same things. They can also support our mission!"

Michael sat back in his seat and smiled. "Now you get it. Yes, you got it. You are a very quick learner, Joe. So what I want you to do is create: 1) a mission statement for the company, 2) a list of one-, two-, and three-year goals for the company, and 3) a list of goals for yourself. Here is the difference: you may set a revenue goal for the company and then set a personal, financial goal for yourself. One is for the company and one is for you. This exercise helps you figure out where you want to be in the next year, two years, or three years. It can be a powerful motivator, and it increases the clarity of your thinking. You can't hit a target if you don't know what it is. This is not an easy task and requires some deep thinking on your part. As Henry Ford once said, 'Thinking is the hardest work there is, which is probably the reason why so few engage in it.'"

Joe looked at Michael and said, "That is so true and such great advice. I am curious, how did you learn all this, Michael?"

"I have always made a commitment to reading and studying all my life. I read every day for at least thirty minutes. I have also been very blessed to have had some great teachers in my life, and I listened to them carefully and heeded their good advice."

"Well, Michael, you are a great teacher yourself," said Joe.

"Thanks, Joe—you are very kind. Well, here is my stop coming up. I am looking forward to discussing your progress next time we see each other."

"Thanks so much, Michael. Just so you know, it may sound a little corny, but you are changing my life. I really appreciate it."

"Well, I am glad to hear that because that is my personal mission—to change people's lives. Thanks for telling me. Have a great week, Joe."

CHAPTER THREE

"You too—see you soon."

Later that day, Joe received another email from Michael:

Dear Joe,

It was great speaking with you again today. Your enthusiasm and willingness to learn is outstanding. You are a breath of fresh air, young man! With your spirit and attitude, you will succeed beyond even your own imagination.

I think your future is very bright. Think about and prepare for it now. There really are no limits.

Keep thinking about where you want to be. **Do the work** to write out your mission statement. It is also critical to write out your own and your company's goals for one, two, and three years. After all, you can't hit a target **unless you know** what it is."

Here are some wonderful quotes I thought you might enjoy:

"Outstanding people have one thing in common: An absolute sense of mission."—*Zig Ziglar*

THE GOAL TENDER

"A mission statement is not something you write overnight…But fundamentally, your mission statement becomes your constitution, the solid expression of your vision and values. It becomes the criterion by which you measure everything else in your life."—*Stephen Covey*

Until I see you next, keep working and dreaming. It will happen.

Your friend,

Michael

CHAPTER FOUR

Thinking of possibilities is like driving a car on a freeway. You have an open road that stretches endlessly before you where your thoughts are not shackled. But when we say "impossible," we have already reached a dead-end in our minds. So dwell on possibilities to open up your horizon.

—PANKAJ PATEL

The train rattled along the track, and Joe looked out from his favorite window seat at the thin blanket of white snow that had fallen the night before. It was only a few inches, not enough to shut anything down, but enough to make the view look like a classic Andrew Wyeth landscape: black-and-blue-hued tree bark contrasted with the blurs of white, as the tree trunks jutted out above the snow.

These were the tough commuting mornings with slushy roads, cold weather, gloves and overcoats, long waits on the platform, melting snow, and rock salt. Joe relished the idea of not having to do this commute within one year because the company he was planning was going to be so successful that he could quit his job and finally pursue his passion.

"Good morning, Joe."

Joe looked up and saw Michael standing there in a long, black, cashmere coat and with a colorful, black-and-white striped scarf tucked neatly in around his collar. His cheeks were slightly pink from standing in the cold on the train platform.

Michael sat down quickly and dusted the snow off of his shoulders. "Quite a beautiful morning out today, isn't it?"

"Yes," said Joe. "I really like the scenery—it reminds of an Andrew Wyeth painting."

"That is a very good description, Joe. He is one of my favorite painters, I might add. I have always admired his art. There are many of his paintings in a museum not too far from here."

"I will have to check that out," said Joe. "I have not made it there yet."

CHAPTER FOUR

"Well," Michael said. "How is your dreaming and scheming been coming along, young Joe? I bet you have been thinking about many things."

"In a word—fantastic, Michael! You are so right. Some nights I can't go to sleep because I am so fired up! I am very excited, and I already have the first draft of my mission and vision statement done. I also have my main goals written out for one, two, and three years from now."

"That is great news, Joe. I was wondering if you would want to share it with me—that is, if you feel comfortable doing so."

"In fact, Michael, I am very happy to share it with you—I printed you a copy. I will admit, I am excited and nervous about you reading it."

"I am curious—why would you be nervous at all?"

"I don't know," said Joe. "I haven't shown this to anyone else. I don't know if it's right or not. I kind of poured my soul into it. I mean, this is all me on paper…my big dream. I am not even sure if I am making sense here. Do you know what I mean?"

THE GOAL TENDER

"I get it completely," Michael said. "That just means that it is important to you—this really matters. This is your heart and soul and future all in one document. Now you are taking it and handing to another person and saying, 'What do you think of me and my dreams?'"

"Exactly," Joe said.

"So are you going to hand it to me? Do you trust I won't be too harsh of a critic?" Michael held out his hands.

Joe sighed and handed the document to Michael.

"Give me ten minutes."

Joe sat staring out the window of the train. He didn't want to watch Michael reading his mission and vision statement and goals because he didn't want to be overly eager. He also didn't want to see Michael's expressions as he read nor make any prejudgments about what they meant. He was very anxious to hear his feedback and wondered what he was thinking. This was, after all, the first person who had read it.

"OK, I am done." Michael said. "Before I give you any feedback, I want you to know my one rule is my feedback must

CHAPTER FOUR

always be honest, otherwise I am doing the other person a disservice. That is a rule I have always lived by. Understood?"

Joe said, "I want honest feedback. I don't think it is valuable if it isn't true. I will gladly accept any positive or constructive feedback. It's the only way I can improve."

"Joe, I won't keep you in suspense. I am very impressed. This is brilliant and well thought out, and it is obvious to me you put a lot of thought, heart, and effort into it. I will also admit I am a little flattered that you wove one of my ideas into your mission."

"Yes, I did! I remembered what you told me!" said Joe.

"I love the idea of a cookie company that has a great product and wants to spread happiness and joy with its cookies. At the same time, a percentage of sales go to a foundation that helps people who want to start their own business. I love the name, 'The Cookie Jar Fund.'"

"Well you should, Michael," Joe said. "You gave it the name."

Michael nodded. "I had forgotten I gave you that name."

"Now you know why you like it so much." Joe smiled.

"All joking aside, this mission and the idea can be a very successful business. A multimillion-dollar business, in fact."

"Think so?" Joe asked.

"Without a doubt. It's great."

Joe said, "I am so glad you like it. Having read it, how about what can be better?"

"That, Joe, is a very smart question. The sign of a great businessman, or great business woman, in my opinion. Always ask that question—how can it be better? I have, of course, a few ideas. First, I think you are thinking way too small. You must think much bigger."

Joe was a little surprised. "Really?"

"Yes. Let me give you a few examples to think about. First, in your personal goals, you said you want to eliminate all your personal debt and make $200,000 a year by end of year three. That is OK, but why not one million?"

"I guess I didn't want to aim too high."

CHAPTER FOUR

"Why not aim high?"

"I…I…don't know—it just seems a little…umm…too egotistical."

"Joe, listen to me very carefully." Michael paused and held up one finger to make his point. "There is a thin line between being confident and being arrogant or egotistical. Being confident is a necessity. There is nothing wrong in believing in your dreams. If you don't, others won't follow you. You as the founder have to think really big! If you read *Think and Grow Rich* by Napoleon Hill, you will learn that the biggest factor in financial success is being willing to think bigger and bolder. It all starts here first." He took his index finger and slowly tapped his temple.

"I guess you are right."

Michael said, "It is not your fault—maybe you haven't had exposure to big thinking in your life. You may also have had people who have given you negative ideas about wealth and money in your life. You must ignore all those messages and move forward. Don't let people who think small hold you back from thinking big. Think of all the people who have started businesses and the first thing they hear is 'Boy, that sounds risky' and 'You know how many businesses fail in the first five years?' As a Goal Tender, you will need to deflect and block negative comments and limitations on your thinking. If you don't, those voices will squash your dreams before they even come to life."

"You are so right," said Joe. "But I will take responsibility for that. In my life I have allowed that to happen. There have been people who have influenced me to think small. But that ends today."

"Very good, young man. Now that is the spirit—nice job! The other feedback is along the same lines. You say somewhere in this document that you want the company to be 'the premier cookie online retailer in the region.' Why not in the United States or the world? How about the number one cookie company in the world? Let's say you meet with investors. Do they want to invest in the largest cookie company in the region or the US? I think the choice is obvious. I mean, there are many companies that started out regionally and then grew into national brands."

"I agree," Joe said. "If we are going to go for it, let's go big."

Michael said, "I think at the root of the issue, if I had to hazard a guess, is you are not sure of three things: 1) Do you want to be a multimillionaire? 2) Do you believe you deserve it? 3) Do you believe it is possible?"

CHAPTER FOUR

Joe scratched his chin and shook his head up and down slowly. "First of all, those are some really great questions and ones I need to think deeply about. My initial impression is that, yes, I very much want to be a multimillionaire. I have given it a lot of thought lately, and it's not just for the money but for the freedom. When you have money, you have so many more choices. There are more options available when there isn't as much of a restriction on money and resources."

"True."

"On the other questions—I think I need to work on getting beyond my limited thinking. The best way to explain that is I was raised in a household with parents who are great people, salt of the earth, and very hard workers. They are truly the nicest people you could ever meet. But I realize now that they often talked about rich people being greedy or unhappy. They said when people became wealthy, they lost their souls and then had to spend all their time managing their money. If one of my brothers or sisters talked about wanting to be famous or rich, that idea was shot down. I don't really think any of those things, but I do think I have limitations on my thinking because I heard it for so long. I think that experiences can create a mindset that fears success. I can think I want to be wealthy, but in the back of my mind, I am thinking of the negative result of success. I need to be really aware of that kind of thinking. There really are no negatives with success."

"Well, Joe, that is great that you realize it. Now you can start to work on changing your thinking."

"Yes, you are right, Michael. Any ideas on how to do that?"

"Sure. First, keep looking at your goals, mission, and vision every single day. Try to visualize them actually happening. Second, every day try to consume some inspirational content from books, articles or videos. This helps you to keep learning and growing. Third, find highly motivated, optimistic people to hang around with. Lastly, if you have anyone in life you are close to who is negative, don't pay them any attention. Your mind has negative thoughts stored in there, and we are trying to push them out with the positive. I have a quote here from Bruce Lipton, which is fascinating." He dug in his coat pocket and pulled out a slip of paper. "Here it is. Read it out loud, if you don't mind."

Joe took the paper and read it. It said, "Our thoughts are mainly controlled by our subconscious, which is largely formed before the age of 6, and you cannot change the subconscious mind by just thinking about it. That's why the power of positive thinking will not work for most people.

CHAPTER FOUR

The subconscious mind is like a tape player. Until you change the tape, it will not change."

Joe looked up at Michael. "So my tapes need to be re-recorded!"

"Or, just maybe, some of them erased." Michael smiled warmly. "The techniques we just talked about will help you do that, Joe. The interesting thing is many people are not even aware they are thinking like that, much less what to do to change it."

"Wow, Michael, that is such an amazing point, and it tells me I have lots of things to work on, but I am willing to do the work."

Michael smiled. "Yes, I know that, and that is a great trait—being willing to work on yourself."

"Thanks," Joe said. "I really appreciate your time and your encouragement."

"You are very welcome," Michael said. "This is my stop. I will send you an email later today."

"Great," Joe said. "Have a great week."

THE GOAL TENDER

Later that day, Joe received an a email from Michael:

Dear Joe,

It was such a breath of fresh air to speak with you today. In today's world there are so many negative people, and it is great to see you excited and optimistic about your future.

Keep looking over the questions that we talked about:

1) Do you want to be a multimillionaire?

2) Do you believe you deserve it?

3) Do you believe it is possible?

I think if you can answer these questions, you will really cultivate the thought processes necessary for success.

Here are a few quotes you may find helpful:

"The past, like the future, is indefinite and exists only as a spectrum of possibilities." —*Stephen Hawking*

CHAPTER FOUR

"It's not only moving that creates new starting points. Sometimes all it takes is a subtle shift in perspective, an opening of the mind, an intentional pause and reset, or a new route to start to see new options and new possibilities."—*Kristin Armstrong*

I look forward to seeing you on the train again soon.

Your friend,

Michael

CHAPTER FIVE

All who have accomplished great things have had a great aim, have fixed their gaze on a goal which was high, one which sometimes seemed impossible.

—ORISON SWETT MARDEN

It was yet another morning, on yet another train commute into the city for Joe. It was odd how after a few years the mornings became silver blurs, and the evenings just became a tiring last leg home before collapsing on the couch in front of the TV. He wondered how many round trips back and forth he had taken. He also chuckled to himself because he thought the people that ran his regional train should offer a frequent rider program. Surely he would be at gold or platinum status by now. The bad news is the rewards would be more rail travel!

He felt like the last week had been an amazing week—he felt as if his mind and thoughts had been significantly expanded, as if by magic. He had been reading and studying how to get past and change his limiting thinking. It was like he had lived in a very small town and then saw New York City—and had suddenly realized there was a big, amazing world out there. His thinking was not going to be limiting any more—but expansive, bigger, and bolder.

He had lunch with a longtime friend of his and told him what he was planning, and the friend looked at him in a funny way, like he was kind of crazy. He then realized that there were many people who would not understand the new way he was thinking. They kind of liked the "old Joe" better. He realized they were still thinking small, still living in that small town, but he had moved on now. That was OK. He didn't judge—that was their choice and their life—but he was going to reach his full potential.

He had reflected on Michael's questions for many hours, and it helped him gain clarity.

"Well, it looks like they let just about anyone on this train." Michael stood there, smiling.

Joe smiled back and reached over the seat to shake his hand vigorously. "It is great to see you, Michael! You are looking very dapper."

"You too! It is great to see you. So give me an update on what you are up to, Mr. Joe." Michael adjusted his cufflinks.

CHAPTER FIVE

"Well, Michael, I am doing great! I have been reading several books on changing my mindset. I have been devouring them."

"That is wonderful news. You are such a great student, Joe; you have that thirst for knowledge. So in your mind, what would you say you learned in your reading?"

"Well, to use an analogy, it feels like a giant door has opened in my brain. When I open the door, I can now see all the possibilities in front of me. I have never thought this way before. It's like a miracle how my thinking had expanded. I don't know why that door wasn't open before."

Michael smiled. "You didn't have the key before! But you worked hard and went and found several keys. So I guess the idea of an open mind has new meaning for you now."

"Yes!" Joe said. "I have never thought of it that way before. I had a closed mind that prevented me from seeing the possibilities."

Michael nodded, saying, "It is very exciting when you see the possibilities and realize there are so many opportunities available to you. There really are no limitations."

THE GOAL TENDER

"Yes, you are right. I am glad you are here today. I had something I wanted to ask you about—I ran into an old friend recently, and we had lunch."

"OK." Michael smiled with a knowing look on his face. He had a feeling he knew what the question was going to be.

"Well we started talking, and I told him about my plans for my business and my goals, and he had an odd reaction to what I told him. I will admit I didn't expect it. He gave me 'that look.' I am sure you know the look I mean. It was almost as if he thought I was crazy for thinking in this new way, and he wanted the old, 'limited thinking' Joe back. He then proceeded to tell me all the reasons why my idea wouldn't and couldn't work. When I told him why my idea would work, he got a little irritated. What was that all about, in your view? It was very puzzling and disappointing."

Michael chuckled softly and shook his head. "Ah yes, the arrival of the naysayers! Remember several weeks ago when we talked about ESVs? As in Energy Sucking Vampires? That is what they do. For some reason—and I don't know why—some people who are limited in their thinking try to get people to *conform* to *their* limited view of the world. They actually get upset if your view doesn't meld with theirs. It's almost like you aren't following the 'rules,' and for some

CHAPTER FIVE

reason that bothers them. It is also ironic that some people who know you *want* you to remain the old version of you. When you start to grow and become the new version of you, they don't like it. They are somehow threatened by the new you."

Joe shook his head. "But why, Michael? Maybe I am being naïve, but why wouldn't they just be happy for me?"

Michael held up a hand and swept it across his body. "I completely agree, and true friends, real friends, will be glad for you. But some people are either jealous of or threatened by the new you because you show them their own limitations. You are holding up a mirror that reminds them of what they haven't achieved. But as we have discussed, you must ignore them and only associate with positive, upbeat, and optimistic people who support you and believe in your dream."

"Very true. I have also been thinking about the three questions from last time, and I have answers to all of them." Joe reached in his briefcase and pulled out his journal. "1) Do you want to be a multimillionaire? Yes. 2) Do you believe you deserve it? Why not me? 3) Do you believe it is possible? I believe it is possible, and I know that because of the reactions I have received every time someone tastes one of my cookies."

THE GOAL TENDER

Michael smiled and said, "Superb, Joe. You have done the work to get your mindset just right and where it needs to be. So what now, Mr. Joe?"

"That is just what I was going to ask you—that very question," Joe said.

"You are ready for the next step. Now that you have your goals in place, it is time to execute them. This is the next, most important step in being a Goal Tender. I call it 'prioritize and calendar-ize.'"

"How does that work?" Joe asked. He had his journal in his hand and a pen to take notes.

"It is deceptively simple. Make a list of all the things you need to do to get your empire built. Once that list is made, then 1) decide on priorities—which one needs to be done first, second, third, etc. and 2) calendar-ize them. That means to take out your paper or electronic calendar and put every task on the calendar as far as one year out. Then every Sunday night or Monday morning, you look at the tasks you need to get done that week to achieve the goals. I have found that unless something is on the calendar, it just never gets done."

CHAPTER FIVE

"Prioritize and calendar-ize," Joe said, looking thoughtfully at what he had written down. "So what this really is, is looking at what we need to do first, and then when we are going to do it."

"That is a smart way of looking at it, Joe. I meet lots of people who don't have goals, so they don't know what they are going to do. I also meet people who have goals but don't put them on the calendar and, therefore, never get them done. So the first person doesn't know where they are going because they don't have a map, and the second person knows where they are going, but they don't know when they are going. I saw a great quote about goals this morning in my reading." He pulled out his journal and flipped to a page. "Ah, here it is—this one is really profound: 'It must be borne in mind that the tragedy of life doesn't lie in not reaching your goal. The tragedy lies in having no goals to reach.' That was said by Benjamin E. Mays; he was one of the leaders of the American Civil Rights Movement. So it is tragic when people squander their potential, in my mind. When someone dies, it is tragic. To me, even more tragic is if they died without living up to their true potential."

"That is a fascinating way of looking at it," said Joe. "What I find interesting is those same people probably wouldn't go on vacation without making reservations. They would plan out what they want to do on vacation to make the trip count."

Michael said, "Here is the irony—they will spend all that time on planning a **one-week vacation** but won't plan out their life!"

"Why?"

"That is a thoughtful question, Joe. I have my theories about that." Michael thoughtfully scratched his chin. "I think it is a tremendous amount of work to think all that through. Setting goals takes discipline of thought and effort. It is laborious being a **Goal Tender**, but it pays off. I also think some people are afraid if they write down their goals, they will have to be accountable to themselves. They don't want to fail although they failed anyway—they just didn't know it. I also believe some people—as odd as this sounds—don't really know where to start and how to go about doing it. They are a bit overwhelmed. But that puzzles me because today there are so many books, online articles, video tips, and training programs about how to do that."

"I agree the internet is so very helpful. I have found a lot of resources online," Joe said.

CHAPTER FIVE

"The information is within the reach of a button today," Michael said.

Joe said, "Well, I guess I have some work to do. I need to write out my list and prioritize and calendar-ize."

"Very good, Joe. My proverbial stop is arriving soon. I will send you an email to read over, if they are not boring you to death."

"No, Michael, not at all. In fact, they are an extremely helpful summary. I print them out and review them."

"Perfect."

"See you soon, Michael."

After Michael got off the train, Joe had a few more stops to go. He sat looking out the window and thought about how far he had come in such a short time and how lucky he was to have met Michael. Who knew that day would change his life? It was an incredible streak of luck, or maybe he was ready for a lesson and a teacher appeared. Either way, he had a spring in his step because he had a plan and he was creating the blueprint for a business that would buy his freedom. He

THE GOAL TENDER

walked from the train station to his office with a smile of satisfaction.

Later that day, the email arrived from Michael, as always:

Dear Joe,

Thanks for a most fascinating discussion on the train today. Please know that I was not being critical or judgmental about people who don't set goals. It is more about me wanting people to live to their potential (not waste it) and use their God-given talents.

You are doing great, and make sure to stay at it!

Here are some quotes I thought you might appreciate:

"Everyone has inside of him a piece of good news. The good news is that you don't know how great you can be! How much you can love! What you can accomplish! And what your potential is!"
—*Anne Frank*

"Never underestimate the power of dreams and the influence of the human spirit. We are all the same in

CHAPTER FIVE

this notion: The potential for greatness lives within each of us."—*Wilma Rudolph*

See you again soon on a morning train sometime. I always so enjoy our conversations and your unbridled enthusiasm.

Most Sincerely,

Your Friend,

Michael

CHAPTER SIX

Whether you write down your to-do lists in a notebook or use a tool like Evernote, to-do lists can be a real lifesaver, since it reduces the stress of trying to remember things like a meeting or what you need to pick up at the grocery store.

—JOHN RAMPTON

Joe was on his morning train, hurtling down the tracks on the way to his office downtown. This was not a typical morning, however; he felt so different than the way he used to feel. It was such an amazing feeling. His feeling was one of hope and optimism, instead of pessimism about being stuck in a stale job. He knew he had a bright future; he was excited about it. It was just a matter of time before he would be leaving. Yes, he was now in *charge* of his life. He already looked forward to the meeting he would have with his boss. He had played the video several times in his head of what it would be like. He would present his official letter of resignation. His boss would ask who he was leaving to work for, assuming he was leaving to work for another company or even a competitor. He would proudly say he was not leaving for another company; he was leaving because his company had grown so much that he needed to run it full time. He would thank his boss for all the company had done for him. The company had been very good to him and supported him with good work and good pay for years; it was just time to live his dream and go for it. He was ready to move onto the next phase of his life, and he wished them well.

He had been working very hard on his "to-do list" and marked each item in terms of priority. He had worked on posting it on his calendar. Just the act of making the list and "calendar-izing it" made it so much more tangible and real. He also found he was much more focused and was getting much more done.

He looked up and saw Michael walking toward him. He smiled broadly and gave a small wave.

Michael got to the seat and said, "Good morning, Joe! It's great to see you!"

"It's great to see you as well, Michael. You know, I always enjoy meeting with you. You always have great ideas and thoughts during our conversations. I wanted to thank you for taking such an interest in my success."

CHAPTER SIX

"Well, Joe, the pleasure is all mine, especially since you are such an eager student and apply everything right away."

"Michael, why wouldn't I if I want to be successful?"

Michael chuckled. "Not many people do. If I may be frank, some people get good advice and choose to ignore it. I don't really know why—there are probably many complex reasons why people don't want to take advice or seek success, but let's not focus on the negative on this beautiful day. So what has my prize student been up to lately?"

"I have many things to share that I am excited about."

"Great. I was thinking about you this weekend and was curious how you were doing. Please don't keep me in suspense!"

Joe reached into his briefcase and pulled out his hardbound book. It had something written on the front cover. He flipped over a few pages. "Ah yes, here is the list. This is a list of all the things I need to do to get my business up and running. Would you like to see it?"

"Sure, Joe!" Michael read over the list. "Well, I must say this is very impressive." He had a look on his face of pleasant surprise.

"Thanks," said Joe. "Just to explain—I made the list, and then I want back and gave each one a number. Ones are urgent—I need to do those tasks ASAP. Twos are things I need to do, and threes are things that need to be done but are not as urgent and require some kind of research or pre-work. For example, I need to get a license with the state to do business, but I also have to research the rules and regulations about baking cookies in my house, at least at first. Later, of course, I will make them in a commercial kitchen."

"Excellent. How do you know when an item on the list is done?"

"Well, I put a checkmark by each item when it is done and write the date of completion."

"That is a very good idea. May I ask a question which may be a little too nosy—you don't have to answer if you don't want to."

"Michael, I trust you. You have earned the right to ask anything."

"I noticed something written on the cover—what is that? I couldn't read it before you opened the book."

CHAPTER SIX

Joe took the book from Michael and flipped over to the front cover. "It says 'Blueprint for my Multimillion Dollar Business.'" It was written in bold, black marker on the green surface of the journal. Joe blushed after he read it.

Michael paused and nodded. "I love it—truer words have never been spoken. I was wondering why you seem a little embarrassed by your title."

Joe squirmed a little in his seat. "Hmm…I guess I have changed my thinking, but every now and then the old me wants to not be so bold. But I don't let myself think it very long."

"I am proud, Joe, that you have been working on that and most importantly on your awareness of it."

"Thanks, Michael. I have really been working on it."

"I read a quote this morning that related to just that. Let me see…" Michael pulled out his book. "Ah yes, this is a good one: 'You can't change who you are, but you can change what you have in your head, you can refresh what you're thinking about, you can put some fresh air in your brain.' That was said by Ernesto Bertarelli. He is a Swiss billionaire."

"That is a good quote, Michael, and a very good point. I have taken action on adjusting my own mindset, but I also have had to change some of the people I associate with. Remember that guy who was so negative about my business? He asked me to have lunch again, and I politely declined. I made a list of the people that I know personally and professionally and determined whether they have negative or positive outlooks. I am spending very little time with the Energy Sucking Vampires and much more time with the positive ones. I also remembered a lady I used to work with, who now works at another company, and who was always so great and positive. I contacted her and we had lunch last week."

"How did that go?"

"It was real eye-opener, I must say. She was very positive and energetic. When I told her about my idea, she supported it and was very excited for me. She then told me about her goal, and I was very supportive of her. I left that meeting more energized than ever."

"My dear Joe, you have discovered a universal truth! I have known this for a long time, and I will admit it was a long, arduous lesson for me to learn. There are ESVs—the Energy Sucking Vampires that take away your energy—but then there are EBCs, and they are *Energy Building Catalysts*. EBCs increase your energy, build you up, and improve

CHAPTER SIX

your thoughts by adding to them. Any time you add a catalyst, there is a positive chemical reaction. A catalyst makes something better, bigger, faster. So the goal then is to have friends and associates who are EBCs. Then you can be an EBC for them."

"Wow! Michael, that is such a great point, and I guess I never thought of it before."

"Not many people do. They just become friends or associate with people because they are fun or interesting. But I think we have to be more conscious of who we associate with. We must, by necessity, be selective. All the successful people that I know associate with other successful people when they can. They choose to associate with positive people as much as they can. It is not snobbery or exclusionary behavior. You are just choosing to be around EBCs instead of ESVs. As supermodel and entrepreneur Heidi Klum once said, 'I think it's important to get your surroundings as well as yourself into a positive state—meaning surround yourself with positive people, not the kind who are negative and jealous of everything you do.'"

"I am very aware of it now, and I am so glad I am."

"Great," said Michael. "That is what exceptional people do. So, have you also started calendar-izing?"

Joe smiled, nodded excitedly, and said, "Yes, I have. That has been really helpful. I have found that when I put it on my calendar, I don't have to remember it anymore. Plus, it comes up on my calendar and reminds me what I have to do."

Michael said, "Well you have made amazing progress, my friend. As you know, if you don't put it on your calendar, it doesn't happen and you forget."

"I have found it to be very powerful. So, Michael, what else should I be doing that I am not doing?"

"Good question, my good man." Michael thought about the question for a few seconds. "I think you are indeed ready for the next step in the process of being a **Goal Tender**. It is what I call *the daily list*. So what you have already created is the master list—it's all the things you have to do. You have also posted them in your calendar. My best advice is to take your master list, and on Sunday night, go through it and write out a weekly list. These are all the things you absolutely have to do this week. They would be what you call your number ones. Then, each day you write out what you need to do personally and professionally. You keep it in front of you every day. This is your daily list for Monday, Tuesday, or Wednesday—whatever day you are getting ready to experience. You just need to get in the habit of doing the daily list."

"Yes, Michael, that makes so much sense."

CHAPTER SIX

"If we look at this from a 30,000-foot view, it looks like this." Michael took out a blank piece of white paper and drew a diagram with circles. "At the top, we have our mission, vision, and yearly goals; then, we have our quarterly, monthly, weekly, and daily goals. Tied to that, then we have our master to-do list and our daily list. The two work together. We set the goals and then create the list of the actions we need to take to achieve them." He handed the paper to Joe.

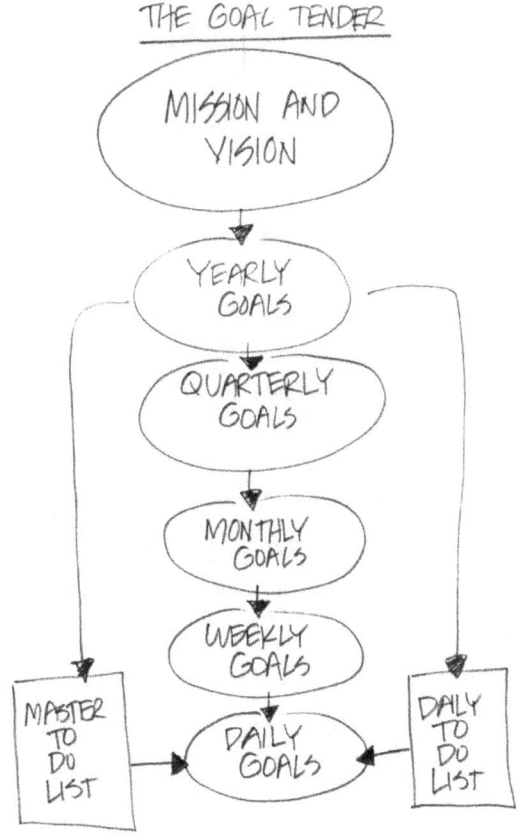

Joe took it and looked it over. He whistled softly.

"Michael, it is so simple and yet so smart and so very clear."

"There is art in simplicity and simplicity in art. It doesn't have to be complicated."

"It's like a whole system where each part is connected to the other," Joe said. "I also realize you are a very good teacher. You have been feeding me one part at a time."

Michael smiled and shrugged his shoulders a little. "I shall not reveal my secrets all at once to my young pupil."

"But is there more?" Joe asked with a curious tone in his voice.

Michael held up his hand toward Joe. "Oh yes, there is more, but all in good time. Take each part and digest it and apply it, and then I will give you the rest."

Joe said, "I am curious, Michael—where did all of this wisdom come from?"

CHAPTER SIX

Michael chuckled softly. "Thank you for the very kind compliment. My wisdom comes from a combination of living life and paying attention to what worked and what didn't. The road of life can be a great teacher if you watch and listen. I guess I am a curious soul. It also came from reading—I have always read at least one book a week. It was also studying, having great mentors, and working for some great and, I might add, some not-so-great leaders in my career. I also married an extraordinary woman who has great brain power and is a great learner too. She has, without a doubt, made me a better man. She has always supported my thinking and ideas, and I have supported hers. We drive and support each other's passions in life."

"That is certainly great to hear," Joe said.

"Well, my stop is coming up. I wish you well and hope you have a great week."

"Thanks, Michael—I plan on it."

After Michael left, Joe grabbed his book and wrote down some of the key points Michael had brought up so he wouldn't forget them. He felt like he was exposed to a man of great wisdom and intelligence. How lucky could a guy get?

THE GOAL TENDER

Later that day, Joe got another email. He always looked forward to reading them.

Dear Joe,

Well, yet another great and stimulating conversation. I think you are a EBC! I am glad you are doing so well on your journey to becoming a business owner. You are well on your way! I am very impressed by your ability to learn and apply it so quickly. You are an amazing student.

Here are some quotes I thought you would enjoy:

"Don't let people disrespect you. My mom says don't open the door to the devil. Surround yourself with positive people."—*Cuba Gooding, Jr.*

"I believe that you should gravitate to people who are doing productive and positive things with their lives."—*Nadia Comaneci*

CHAPTER SIX

"You were born to win, but to be a winner, you must plan to win, prepare to win, and expect to win."
—*Zig Ziglar*

Have an amazing week!

Your friend,

Michael

CHAPTER SEVEN

In many spheres of human endeavor, from science to business to education to economic policy, good decisions depend on good measurement.

—BEN BERNANKE

Joe was on the train, and it was the week heading into Thanksgiving. Joe felt so grateful and thankful for all that had changed. He felt like his attitude and mindset had improved and he was well on his way to having his own business. He had a logo and a business plan and had received his paperwork from the state approving his company name. It felt really real, and he thought that in a few short months, it would be up and running. The website was almost done. He hoped that within one year his business would support him full time. Yes, his cookie company would be a reality. Who knows? He was starting to think he could be the next Mrs. Fields or Famous Amos or Auntie Anne's. It was all possible and within his reach. He knew it and strangely felt it. He believed it, and he saw it in his mind.

He had to admit that his chance meeting with Michael had been a huge influence on him. He realized he just needed someone to encourage and support him. How ironic that what he needed came from a total stranger and one who cared enough to give him advice that was solid! It had changed his life and mindset completely. He was very excited about going into the new year and was excited to see what would happen with his new business.

"Good morning, Mr. Joe." Michael walked up to his row of seats.

"Michael! It is great to see you as always! How are you this morning?"

"I am doing extremely well!" Michael said with enthusiasm. "How is my star pupil doing?"

"Michael, I am doing great. Everything is clicking right along, and I am making great progress. I have a final logo, and I received my paperwork from the state saying my business name for my company had been approved."

Michael nodded. "Well, that is exciting! Congratulations. How does it feel?"

CHAPTER SEVEN

"It is a great feeling," said Joe. "To see it officially in writing is very exciting. It may sound odd, but it is as if my thoughts are now becoming a physical reality. That is really exciting and makes me feel very proud."

"You should be proud. Your hard work and energy are becoming a reality. Are you familiar with the law of attraction?"

"I think I have heard of it. I can't say that I know exactly what it is."

Michael put both hands together and laced his fingers. "It is a theory first talked about in a book back in the late 1800s. Here is the idea: what you think about most is what you *become*. The theory is your mind is like a transmission tower. The signals that you send out attract things to you. Positive thoughts attract positive things; negative thoughts attract negative. People, resources, money, and whatnot can all be drawn to you by the law of attraction. That is the concept in a nutshell. It has been written about in many books, such as *Think and Grow Rich*, *Thoughts are Things*, and *The Secret*. I would argue that you, young man, have been practicing the law of attraction without even knowing it."

"I see," said Joe. "That is really interesting."

"I also think of this as manifestation."

"How do you mean?" asked Joe.

"Well, look out the window at that building—see the white one? That building started out in the mind of someone, an executive or an architect or a builder. Through their vision, their thoughts and actions, it went on paper first and then became the physical manifestation of that. Now we see it, but it started in someone's mind first. I also think that being a **Goal Tender** means applying the law of attraction by thinking about your goals, talking about them with people you trust, putting them in writing, and then doing it by taking action. Then it becomes manifested in physical form. It becomes a reality."

"That makes so much sense. What we think about creates our reality," said Joe. "I have also noticed when people are upbeat and enthusiastic and positive, other people want to be around them and want to work with them. The opposite is also true: when people are very negative, people don't want to be around them—they are a real downer."

"Very true," said Michael. "I have also noticed negative people like to hang out with each other."

"I guess birds of a feather really do flock together?"

CHAPTER SEVEN

"Yes they certainly seem to—because they feel most comfortable hanging out with their own birds," Michael said. "On another note—how are you doing with your daily list tool?"

"Michael, it is going great. I know exactly what I need to do each day and each week. It makes me much more productive and focused."

"Very good, my young protégé," said Michael. "One other advantage you may not have thought about is it helps us also decide what NOT to work on. It helps us prioritize our time."

"That is a great point, Michael. Is there anything else I should be looking at?"

"In fact, there is, and I am glad you asked. It is the idea of measurement and accountability."

"Measurement?" asked Joe.

"Yes," said Michael. "If you are going to have goals, they have to be measured. How do you know whether you are successful if nothing is measured? How can you hold yourself accountable? For example, let's say someone says they want to lose weight."

THE GOAL TENDER

"OK," said Joe.

Michael said, "Then the question becomes: 1) How much weight? 2) By when? 3) How? Or what is the plan? Let's say someone says they want to lose fifty-four pounds. Then they need to say: 1) How much weight? 2) How much each week? 3) What plan will they follow for diet and exercise? The whole point is we now know they are achieving along the way and that when they reach the goal of fifty-four pounds lost, they know they achieved it!"

"Got it," said Joe.

"So I want to look at all your goals and try to figure out if you have measurements on all of them. For example, you are starting a business. Do you have a specific date in mind?"

"I was thinking first quarter of this coming year," Joe said.

Michael smiled and said, "It's kind of like people saying as part of their New Year's resolution that they 'want to get in better shape.' The problem is there is no measurement. So instead of saying first quarter, I would pick an exact date, say like February 28."

"I hadn't thought of that. I guess I am being too vague. That is a very good point, Michael. I guess when I say 'start my

CHAPTER SEVEN

business,' I also have to define what that means. I can say website up and ready to take orders. I need to be precise."

"There you go—now you have it," said Michael.

"I don't know why I didn't think of it before," Joe said.

"Don't be too hard on yourself. The most important part is you know it now," Michael said.

"Wow," Joe said. "I am going to go back to all of my goals that are written and add in the dates and measurements."

"Excellent. Well, we are coming up on my stop soon. I certainly hope you have a wonderful and blessed Thanksgiving."

"You too, Michael," Joe said. "I am very thankful for all your help and advice. It has been invaluable."

"You are most welcome," said Michael. "And I am thankful you are such a good student." Michael rose for his stop.

"Goodbye and Happy Turkey Day," Joe said and shook Michael's hand.

"Goodbye Joe and Happy Thanksgiving to you."

THE GOAL TENDER

After Michael left, Joe was thinking about all Michael had said. He felt like each discussion was a new piece of the puzzle being handed to him—and he was fascinated that all the pieces were falling into place. He was so grateful for the wisdom and perspective Michael provided.

He was ready to review each of his goals and apply measurements and timelines.

Later that day, he received an email from Michael as usual:

Dear Joe,

I am very proud of your progress, and I really enjoyed our conversation today about goals and measurement. You are a super learner.

Here are a few quotes I thought you would enjoy:

"Dates that come around every year help us measure progress in our lives. One annual event, New Year's Day, is a time of reflection and resolution." —*Joseph B. Wirthlin*

"Success has always been easy to measure. It is the distance between one's origins and one's final achievement."—*Michael Korda*

CHAPTER SEVEN

"People who believe they have the power to exercise some measure of control over their lives are healthier, more effective and more successful than those who lack faith in their ability to effect changes in their lives." —*Albert Bandura*

Happy Thanksgiving!

Your Friend,

Michael

CHAPTER EIGHT

Do not wait; the time will never be "just right." Start where you stand, and work with whatever tools you may have at your command, and better tools will be found as you go along.

—GEORGE HERBERT

Joe was back on the train, and it was another blue, cold day. The clouds were low in the sky and looked like they could sprinkle some snow if they decided to—even though there was none in the forecast. Joe smiled when he thought about the weather forecast because it seemed like they were wrong more than half the time anyway. He didn't let weather affect him; he couldn't control it—just his reaction to it.

It was a great day for Joe, even though he was in the middle of the workweek. It didn't matter anymore because he had bigger dreams and ambitions beyond the job. He was in the process of building an empire. He had enjoyed his job in the meantime, but now he was on his way to making his dreams really come true. He wasn't just waiting around for his ship to come in—he was building one and getting ready to launch it. It is a darn fine looking ship, he thought to himself. He looked around the train at all the usual people who commuted every day and thought to himself something amazing—that every person on this train could be future buyers of his product. They could be on this train, having some joy in their day by eating one of his cookies.

Joe had been doing a ton of reading and planning for his new business. He had read the book about Richard Branson and how he started Virgin and then all the other Virgin companies. He found it to be a tremendous source of inspiration and motivation because Branson started with nothing and built an amazing company. Joe had learned many valuable lessons and had been taking notes in his journal as he did his morning reading. It had become a regular part of his routine.

"Well, look who we have here. They do allow gentleman on this train after all." Michael stood there in a dark navy, wool coat with a soft, yellow scarf with black stripes and black leather gloves. He looked like a model for one of those fine men's clothing catalogs.

"Well, good morning, Michael. You are looking very dapper this morning."

CHAPTER EIGHT

"Thanks, Joe. It's very good to see you," Michael said with a smile. He unbuttoned his coat and sat down. "I was thinking about you this morning. I found this article online about a lady who started a donut company. I saw many parallels between you and her. I printed it out for you." He handed the pages to Joe.

"Wow. Thanks so much, Michael. That was so nice of you to think of me and go to that much trouble."

"No trouble at all. I knew you would enjoy it." Michael bowed his head slightly. He coughed a few times and patted his chest. "Sorry, fighting a bit of a chest cold. Nasty buggers. I am feeling much better though."

"Sorry to hear that," said Joe. "I am glad you are feeling better. Thanks for the article. I will add that to my morning reading tomorrow."

"Morning reading? That sounds interesting. Do tell me about that, young Joe."

"Well Michael, I have been reading a great deal, and I made an interesting connection in my reading. Many of the highly successful people I have read about have one interesting thing in common. What they have in common is they all invest some time every morning reading or studying in order to get their mind right and start their day off on the right foot. It's the best way to start your day."

"A very clever observation, Joe. That is so true in my book. I have for many years spent thirty minutes in the morning reading. I also make sure it is not news, which has always been way too negative. I only read something that is constructive, positive, and uplifting. It has been very beneficial, and you are right—it's a great way to start the day."

"Yes, Michael, that is what I have found, and it's a new habit that has become part of my regular routine."

"Great," Michael said. "You have really come a long way, my friend."

"Thanks," said Joe.

"So I am bursting with curiosity. How is everything else going, Joe?"

"I am happy to say things are going great. As you suggested, I took time and sat down and reviewed all my goals. I took each goal and made it measurable. I then looked at each goal and made sure it was time-bound—something I could put on a calendar."

CHAPTER EIGHT

"How did that work for you?" Michael asked, even though he had a pretty good idea of what the answer was going to be.

"I have given that a great deal of thought, and it has helped me so much. I have more focus, and I now have deadlines instead of vague generalities. For example, I decided I could have my business up and running and be selling product by February 28 of next year. As you know, that is only a few months away. But I will be ready!"

"That is the spirit," Michael said.

"Once I have the date set and on the calendar, then I can make a list and work backward from the date. If I know it is February 28, then I am just working everything in reverse from that date. That has helped me gain clarity as to when things need to be done to reach my goal."

"Just superb, Joe. Well played." Michael was giving Joe a slow and quiet golf clap. "I applaud you." He bowed slightly toward Joe.

"Thanks so very much, Michael. You have been a great help. Now that you know all that, is there anything else I am missing? I want to make sure I am as successful as possible."

"Oh, you will be, my lad. You will be very successful, I assure you. There is another element we have not discussed."

"Please share with me," Joe said.

"It is making sure you have systems and processes in place so you can achieve your goals. When I say systems, I mean things that can automate tasks and remind you to do something, like a calendar system, for example. The idea is to set up systems so you can be organized, save time, and be as efficient as possible."

"I think I see what you mean," said Joe.

"OK, let me give you an example. Let say you, Joe, schedule an appointment for a meeting. Where does that appointment go?"

"I post it on my calendar that day," Joe said.

"What kind of calendar?" Michael asked with his finger raised quizzically.

"A paper time management system I use."

CHAPTER EIGHT

"Ah. See, what if that date was also entered in an electronic calendar? Then it would remind you of your meeting ten minutes before it was going to start—and give you the call-in numbers and information. That is what I mean by automation. That reminder would pop up on your laptop, desktop, or smartphone. You don't need to remember it."

"I see," said Joe.

"The other beauty of it is you can invite people to meetings and get on their calendars as the meeting organizer," Michael said. "So then the goal becomes to look at all functions and see which ones can be automated through your smartphone, email, address book, and all other forms of technology."

"I guess I am not big on technology,." Joe said.

"Neither am I, my friend, but I am big on what technology can do if it saves me time, makes me more productive, and, most importantly, frees up my brain power to work on more important things like my goals."

"A very good point, Michael."

"Let me give you some other examples which you may find helpful. First is using phone apps. I can use a phone app to track anything, to remind me of my goals, and to help me break those goals into smaller tasks. For example, if I wanted to run a 5K, it would break it all down and tell me what I needed to do to train. My point is you can find apps to do anything goal-oriented."

"That is great idea, Michael."

"Thanks. You can also use online resources, like LinkedIn or Google groups. Find groups related to the goals you are working on and join them. Then you can have the support of the group and can ask questions and get ideas from its members. Another example is you can use programs for project management. There are lots of programs online you can use to manage projects and to collaborate on projects with a group that are all working on it."

"Wow. I didn't know about any of this," Joe said.

"There is such great technology now, Joe, and more comes out every day. You can even use programs to manage financial goals. So again, much of it can be automated. The great thing about those kinds of programs is they remind you of what you need to do. The items that the programs remind you to do may be tasks you didn't know about. As you build your company, you need to create systems to help you out. It can be technology, a virtual assistant, or tools to manage

CHAPTER EIGHT

your social media." Michael gestured as if he was gathering up everything into his arms.

"Where do I find all of this out?"

"Well Joe, you can buy books on it, watch videos online, or hire a technology consultant for a few hours to help you organize everything. It is amazing what can be done. Imagine for a moment you want to send out social media messages on Twitter every day for your new company. That can all be automated. You create the messages and put them into technology that releases them each day. What I would recommend is constantly reading about technology to see what is new and exciting."

"Wow," said Joe. "Using technology will help me plan, organize, and execute my goals. That is fantastic. I will get to work on that as soon as possible."

"It will be a great help to you," Michael said. "Don't get me wrong. I am not saying technology is as effective as two people talking face-to-face, as we have done the last few months. What I am saying is it can be a valuable tool. As you become busier, systems help you not have to remember." Michael pointed to his temple with his index finger.

"Great point, Michael."

The conductor started calling the next stop, and Michael reflexively stood up, buttoned his coat, and wrapped his scarf around his neck. "This is my stop, as you know. Have a great week."

"You too, Michael," Joe said, and he shook Michael's hand goodbye.

Later that day, it was no surprise—he had an email from Michael:

> Dear Joe,
>
> What a delightful conversation we had today! You continue to grow and amaze me with your progress. I am very proud of how far you have come in such a short time, and I may have had a small part in it.
>
> Here are some quotes I thought you might enjoy:
>
> "You can't cross the sea merely by standing and staring at the water."—*Rabindranath Tagore*
>
> "Learning is the beginning of wealth. Learning is the beginning of health. Learning is the beginning of spirituality. Searching and learning is where the miracle process all begins."—*Jim Rohn*

CHAPTER EIGHT

"I learned that we can do anything, but we can't do everything…at least not at the same time. So think of your priorities not in terms of what activities you do, but when you do them. Timing is everything."
—*Dan Millman*

Your friend,

Michael

CHAPTER NINE

Visualize this thing that you want, see it, feel it, believe in it. Make your mental blue print, and begin to build.

—ROBERT COLLIER

Joe was back in his usual seat on his regional railcar, heading off to work yet again. Looking out the window, he saw the colorful Christmas lights that went by in a blur of dancing red and blue and green. He always loved the lights this time of year.

He was right on track with the launch of his company in February. He was planning on taking off a few extra days around the holidays to work on some final details of the company launch. He also had found some suppliers of ingredients who he wanted to meet with. He was so ready to embrace the New Year because it was going to be an exciting one, and he knew it was going to be life-changing.

He reached into his leather satchel and pulled out his journal. He had been writing in it every day, taking notes from his readings, refining goals, and adding measurable aspects to each one. He would make a note whenever he had a new thought. He liked that people like Leonardo da Vinci and Thomas Edison practiced these habits, just like he was doing now. He also would read and reread the goals each day to reinforce them in his mind. He wondered how many people on the train had goals for the new year. It made him a bit sad to think that many of them didn't. They would not live up to their potential. It suddenly came to him that that used to be him, not so long ago. Not anymore—never again.

"Top of the morning, Mr. Joe." Michael was standing there in a camel hair overcoat with dark brown, leather gloves.

"Michael!" Joe exclaimed. "It is great to see you!"

"It's great to see and be seen!" Michael said as he chuckled. "Especially at my age."

"I am always excited to see you, Michael."

"So how is the future Cookie King doing?" Michael asked.

"I am doing great. Everything is cranking along, and I am ready to launch."

CHAPTER NINE

"Well, that is wonderful news, Joe. Are you ready to become a multimillionaire?"

"I am very excited about the launch. It is going to be great."

Michael furrowed his brow just slightly. "May I ask you a question?"

"Sure," said Joe.

"This is just an observation, but an important one. When I asked if you were ready to be a multimillionaire, you skipped over the question, kind of deflected it."

"Did I?" asked Joe.

"I think so. So I will ask you again—do you want to and are you ready to be a multimillionaire?"

"Sure—uh, I guess," Joe stammered.

"This is an important lesson. You have goals, and they are great ones. But, my young friend, you have to be willing to say, 'I am absolutely ready to be a multimillionaire, and it is going to happen.' Remember we talked about the law of attraction? This mind of yours is the satellite—the question is what signals are you sending?"

Joe sighed. "You are so right, Michael. I guess I need to be much more aware of what I am saying."

"Good, Joe. You know there is an element we haven't discussed, and that is the issue of fear. Are you ever fearful that your new venture will fail? Ever roll over in bed late at night and think about that?"

"Well, I do think of it every now and then, if I am being honest, but I know I can't be successful if I don't take a risk. As the old saying goes, no risk, no reward. So I think positively and keep moving forward. I am aware that I need to stay focused on the positive outcome."

"Exactly on point, Joe. More importantly, it is what you are saying to yourself. It sounds funny, but what you say to yourself is what you believe," Michael said. "It becomes your truth."

"Gosh, Michael, that is such a good point. It is just something I need to continue to work on. Do you have any suggestions on what I can do to work on it further?"

CHAPTER NINE

"Well Joe, many of the things we have already talked about you can keep doing—like writing out your goals in your journal, reading positive books and articles, and avoiding negative people. There are a few other things you can do, but they require an open mind."

Joe smiled and pointed at his temple. "I am wide open!"

"OK, have you ever heard of a vision board?" Michael asked.

"No."

"Well, it is a great tool you can use. There are two versions—a physical board or an electronic one. For the physical one, you simply make a board out of cardboard or canvas and paste pictures of things you want. It could be a picture of a mansion, a car, a cookie company, an exotic vacation. They are visual pictures of your goals. That is good if you like doing that kind of activity. For option two, you can take the more modern approach and do the same thing electronically. You can use an app on your phone or iPad and build a vision board you can see on that device every day. You look at it every day to visualize your goals. You can even put a picture of one million dollars on your vision board. Many highly successful people have them."

"Interesting—I will definitely try it," said Joe. "I wonder why it works so well?"

"Most experts think it has to do with your RAS—reticular activating system. When you see it, it activates part of your brain and drives the image into your subconscious mind. Your brain is then working on it all the time."

"Pretty incredible. It's amazing how powerful our minds can be," Joe said.

"I think we have only begun to scratch the surface on what our minds are capable of doing," Michael said. "There are a few other suggestions I have in mind you can try. Have you ever heard of affirmations?"

"I have heard of them, but I'm not sure what they are."

"Affirmations are simply written or spoken statements of what you want, stated in the present form, as if you have already accomplished them. You state 'I, Joe, am the owner of my own company, and I have generated over one million dollars in revenue.' Most experts say to write them out over and over every day. They also say you should say them out loud each day. In fact, I read a recent study from Carnegie

CHAPTER NINE

Mellon that reveals that self-affirmations can protect against the damaging effects of stress, help with problem-solving performance, and counteract ego-depletion."

"Why?"

"It is very effective for changing your thinking. Repetition makes a shift in the way you think. The main thing when you write or say them is to believe they are coming true."

"That makes perfect sense." said Joe. "I guess if something negative has been said by others or by you all your life, then you need to repeat affirmations to overcome the thoughts you have in your head."

"There is the famous story about the actor Jim Carrey," said Michael. "When he was just starting out and was a broke, out-of-work actor and comedian, he wrote out a check to himself for ten million dollars. He put it in his wallet and carried it everywhere with him. On the memo line he wrote 'for acting services,' and he dated it for five years later. He looked at it every day. Five years later, he was paid ten million dollars to star in a movie. So this is an example of a great form of affirmation. I kind of think of it as reprogramming your internal computer. Out with the old apps and in with the new."

"I love that," said Joe.

"How do you feel about saying affirmations out loud?" asked Michael.

"I am sure there will be a learning curve, and it may be odd at first. But I am definitely willing to try. I need to have the right mindset. My sister is a black belt in martial arts and she told me a lot of what they do is not only physical but mental. They can do many of the things they do because they have the right mindset."

"Good man. You are always willing to try," Michael said.

"Why would I listen to experts and then choose to ignore them? That would be silly, " Joe said.

"Well Joe, some people stubbornly cling to their old beliefs because they are comfortable. But staying in their comfort zone does not allow them to grow. You have to be willing to take risks. As Frank Scully once said, 'Sometimes you have to go out on a limb because that is where the fruit is.' As the saying goes, old habits die hard. Joe, if you want to be successful—and I know you will be—you must change your habits and, most importantly, change the way you think. You already have in many ways."

CHAPTER NINE

"Thanks, Michael. I have had a great teacher." He smiled. "In all sincerity, I really appreciate your wisdom and advice."

"You are very welcome, Joe," Michael said. "It is great to coach someone when they are so eager to learn."

"I am going to work on all the items we talked about today. Many of them I was not aware of at all," Joe said.

"Great. I see my stop is fast approaching. I hope you have a great week. Just remember, change your mind, change your destiny!"

"Who said that?" asked Joe.

"I did!" Michael turned and laughed as he walked down the train aisle to his exit door.

Joe sat thinking about how lucky he was to have Michael as a mentor and a teacher. He had to think about something he could give him, some gift as a gesture of his appreciation. He had learned so much, and today's discussion felt like another very important step in his journey.

THE GOAL TENDER

He opened up his journal and wrote down some of the key points Michael had mentioned, before his stop came up and he had to pack up his stuff.

Later that day, Joe got an email from Michael:

Dear Joe,

I must say our conversations on the train continue to delight me and get me thinking. It is such a pleasure to speak with you and talk about all these great ideas.

You remind me of myself when I was your age, before I learned how to think just a little bit differently. I think you have a tiger by the tail, Joe—you really do—and you will be very successful.

Here are few quotes I thought you would enjoy:

"Success is no accident. It is hard work, perseverance, learning, studying, sacrifice and most of all, love of what you are doing or learning to do."—*Pelé*

"If you always put limit on everything you do, physical or anything else. It will spread into your work

CHAPTER NINE

and into your life. There are no limits. There are only plateaus, and you must not stay there, you must go beyond them." —*Bruce Lee*

"Someone is sitting in the shade today because someone planted a tree a long time ago." —*Warren Buffett*

Your friend,

Michael

CHAPTER TEN

You are the sum total of everything you've ever seen, heard, eaten, smelled, been told, forgot—it's all there. Everything influences each of us, and because of that I try to make sure that my experiences are positive.

—MAYA ANGELOU

Joe was back on the train and was very excited because today was a very special day. He was taking the day off to visit Michael at his office. He had been surprised because he had received an email invitation last week. The email read as follows:

Hello Joe,

Allow me to introduce myself via email. My name is Larry Jackson, and I work with Michael in his office. He wanted me to reach out to you to ask you to come to his office on Tuesday of next week around 10:00 A.M. He has a few things he wanted to share with you and would be very pleased if you could

THE GOAL TENDER

make it. Please let me know if this works for you. Once you confirm, I will forward you the address of our office. When you arrive, please ask for me.

Sincerely,

Larry Jackson

He wondered what it was that Michael wanted to share with him, and he was very curious. He had also been thinking about everything Michael had taught him, and he was so excited about all he was learning that he realized with regret that he really hadn't asked Michael anything about himself. He had been too fired up and involved with his own goals and dreams that he realized he hadn't asked Michael about his goals and dreams. He felt guilty about that and realized he knew nothing about Michael or his family, or what he even did for a living. He just knew he was smart, intelligent, and charming and gave great advice. He seemed successful based on the kind of clothes he wore—they were always the finest and so well-tailored. Other than that, he really knew nothing at all. He was going to make sure to change that today. For today's meeting, he had carefully picked out his best suit and tie and the stylish new dress shoes he just bought last month. He wore his best wristwatch, the one his parents had gotten him when he had received his MBA.

CHAPTER TEN

He had come a long way and was only one month away from the launch, and everything was set. He was ready to be a multimillionaire. His confidence had increased, and he had a great attitude because of the bright future he had planned. He was filled with hope. The irony was that his company gave him a promotion for the New Year, and he was now making more money and had increased responsibility. It was almost as if they sensed he was going to leave even though he had smartly said nothing to anyone at work about his plans. The better job was great for now, but he still planned on leaving once his new company reached certain benchmarks in revenue. He was looking forward to sharing the good news with Michael.

The conductor came through the car, screaming the name of the next stop even though he could have announced it on the intercom system. "Next stop: 30th Street Station…30th Street Station is the next stop. Please take all your belongings, including children, and depart out the door just ahead. Watch the gap as you step off folks! Don't want to lose anyone today!" A few new passengers smiled at the conductor's attempt at humor, but the veteran riders had heard it all before and had no reaction at all.

Joe got off the train and breathed in the cold, fresh morning air, and it was a nice feeling because he wasn't going to work, but to visit a friend. No work or office for him today. No, today it was just some good, thoughtful conversation where he would get to know Michael better. It was going to be a great day.

Joe pulled out the address he had written down and confirmed he was in front of the right building. The sleek, glass tower rose up in the blue sky, an imposing monolith of silver glass with a bright, shiny, aluminum skin that spiral wrapped around the building. It was an architectural marvel. At the top of the building, a huge blue and silver sign read "MMR Industries." Joe smiled and walked to the entrance, pushed through the door, and looked up at the huge cavernous lobby, which was very modern and had white, leather chairs in the waiting area.

Joe walked up to the security desk and waited in a short line. When it was his turn, he walked up to the desk.

"Hello, sir." The blue-suited, broad-shouldered security guard said with a deep voice of authority.

"Good morning!" said Joe. "I am here to see Larry Jackson, please."

The security guard's eyebrows went up a notch. "Do you have an appointment?"

CHAPTER TEN

"Yes, I do," said Joe. "For 10:00 o'clock."

"Hmm—OK," the guard said. "Can I get your ID please?"

"Sure." Joe opened his wallet and handed him his driver's license.

"Tough day to meet with Larry. He ain't having a good day," the guard said, shaking his head slowly side to side.

"Oh...I'm sorry to hear that," Joe said reflexively. The guard had no reply.

"Sir, here is your badge—and ID back. Keep that displayed on the outside of your jacket at all times. Please be seated in our waiting area, and Mr. Jackson will come and take you up."

"Thanks. Have a good day, sir," Joe said.

"I will try, man," the guard said, shaking his head again.

Joe went over and sat in one of the white leather and chrome seats facing the elevators so that he could see when Mr. Jackson arrived in the lobby. He was early; it was only 9:45 and his appointment was at 10:00.

After about fifteen minutes, a tall, well-tailored man came across the lobby and made direct eye contact with him. His eyes were very blue against a dark olive complexion and dark brown hair.

"Joe?"

"Yes, Mr. Jackson, it is so nice to meet you."

"You too. But please, call me Larry. Please follow me, and I will take you up."

They got on the elevator, and Larry swiped his badge and pressed the button for the fiftieth floor. The elevator lifted off with a whisper but at a very high speed.

"How was your travel in?" Larry asked.

"Great! The train ran on time, which is always good thing," Joe said.

"OK well, we are at our floor. I will see you to the conference room now."

CHAPTER TEN

They entered the conference room. In the middle sat a huge marble conference table—big enough to seat at least twenty people.

"Why don't you sit here?" Larry gestured to a chair. "Would you like spring water or coffee of some sort?"

"Oh no, thank you. I am good," Joe said.

Larry Jackson sat down at the table across from Joe and looked very pensive. He rubbed his forehead lightly. He sighed.

"Well…I am afraid I have some very bad news." Larry looked at Joe with an expression of sadness.

"OK." Joe felt a drop in the pit of his stomach.

"Michael passed away a week ago," Larry said.

"What—oh my God," Joe said.

"Michael passed way after a long battle with cancer, and he was only 74. The entire company is in shock."

"Wait—uh…the *entire company knows* Michael?" Joe asked with a puzzled tone.

"Oh, I am sorry, you didn't know. Michael was the founder of our company and chairman of the board."

"What?" asked Joe in shock.

"The letters on the top of the building are his initials—Michael Mann Redmond Industries—MMR. It's a 50 billion dollar company with over 90,000 employees and offices in twenty countries," Larry patiently explained.

"Your chairman of the board…rode the train?" Joe looked at Larry like this was some joke.

"Michael was always Michael, never Mr. Redmond. I worked with him for twenty years. He was always modest and down to earth. He liked riding the train. He was humble, a real gem of a man, and will be very missed by all of us," Larry said.

"Yes. Me too," Joe said. "I didn't even know he was sick; he was so cheerful and upbeat."

"He always was." Larry cleared his throat and shifted in his seat and sighed.

CHAPTER TEN

"I am sorry you thought you were meeting with Michael today, but he wanted me to tell you in person. He left instructions."

"I understand," Joe said.

"There is, however, another reason you are here today, Joe. I have something for you that Michael wanted delivered to you in person. He gave me this a few weeks ago—I guess he knew the end was near." Larry held out a white, sealed envelope. "It is a letter from him. Please read it here and take all the time you need. I going to put my number on this piece of paper. Just call me when you have read it and are ready. I have a few more things to cover with you. Please take your time."

Larry rose quietly and walked out, shutting the door behind him.

Joe sat very still for a long time, just looking at the envelope in front of him. On the front, in neat handwriting in blue ink, it said, "To my friend Joe."

He couldn't believe Michael was gone. He couldn't believe he had been mentored by the chairman of a 50 *billion dollar company*, and he couldn't believe he had never mentioned it. I mean, how many people in the world would have wanted to sit down that many times with someone like Michael and get advice? He was so lucky. At the same time, he also felt very sad that he didn't get to know him better. Now he was gone. He shook his head.

The envelope still sat there unopened. Michael picked it up and carefully opened the seal. The letter was handwritten in flowing black ink, like it had been written with a fountain pen.

Dear Joe,

If you are reading this, then I am no longer around. I am hopefully attending a meeting in an even more beautiful place.

Joe, I am sorry I didn't tell you that I had a terminal illness. I just knew it would overshadow our conversation, and I wanted to focus on you and your business. I wanted to focus on living, not dying.

I didn't get a chance to say a final goodbye, but I suppose this letter will serve that purpose. However poorly it may do that, I suppose it will suffice. I could have recoded a video, but I guess I am still a bit old-fashioned.

CHAPTER TEN

As a gesture of respect, I asked Mr. Jackson to get this to you so that it would not get lost, and you didn't think I just vanished or wondered why you didn't see me on the train.

There some very important things I would like to pass on to you.

1) It was such a delight and privilege getting to know you and coaching you. You are a great student, and I must say I saw in you the same spark I had years ago when I started my company.

2) You may think that I just helped you, but I took great joy in sharing ideas with you and seeing them put into play so quickly. You brought me joy.

3) You will be very, very successful with your company, and you will be a multimillionaire. You have a great idea, talent, and the right attitude and mindset.

4) Make sure to keep learning every day, and you will keep growing.

THE GOAL TENDER

5) Every year, before the year starts, write down your goals for every area of your life. You must continue to be a Goal Tender, tending to your goals daily.

6) As my legacy, I am asking that you pass on these tools and techniques of being a Goal Tender to as many people as possible. Pass on the torch! There are so many people in the world that could be and do so much more and are not living up to their full potential.

Don't fret about me, Joe.

I lived a great life and achieved all my dreams, even beyond what I could have imagined, and I leave a great company that will contribute much to the world and support many employees and their families for years to come.

Your friend,

Michael

Joe sat with the letter and then folded it and put it back in the envelope. What an amazing letter from an amazing man.

CHAPTER TEN

Afterward, he called Mr. Jackson, who came right way and had more documents in his hand along with a gift bag.

"Hello Joe, are you OK?"

"As well as can be expected, I guess." Joe smiled warmly. "Thanks for your help, Larry."

"You are most welcome. I have to tell you—Michael was really impressed by you, Joe. I have another document, and this document basically says he is bequeathing you his entire library of motivational and self-improvement books. There are about a thousand of them. Many are first editions, and many are autographed by the authors. He wanted you to have them because he knew you would read and appreciate them. It is a priceless collection."

"I must say I am honored, but a bit shocked," Joe said.

"Take this document, review it, and return it with a notarized signature. Then we will arrange for the transfer of the books to the location you designate," Larry said. "He also wanted you to have this."

Joe opened the gift bag, and inside was the most handsome, gold Rolex watch Joe had ever seen.

THE GOAL TENDER

"Michael wanted you to have a watch that was in keeping with you being a future successful entrepreneur," Larry said. "It's engraved on the back."

Joe turned over the gold watch, and on the back it said:

To Joe,

The Goal Tender

Your Friend Forever,

Michael M. Redmond

ACTION PLANNER

WELCOME TO THE GOAL TENDER ACTION PLANNER SECTION.

As an author and motivational speaker, I am passionate about not just *learning* something but actually *doing* something. That is what this action planner section is all about.

Simply go back and read a chapter, and then take time to answer the questions for that chapter. Then it's up to you to prioritize and calendar-ize it!

That's it. It's very simple. So what are you sitting here for? Get going—you have some goal tending to do!

ACTION PLANNER

ACTION PLANNER: CHAPTER ONE

Do you have a place to write down your goals (physical or electronic)?

_____
_____
_____
_____
_____

Do you write your goals down? If not, why not?

_____
_____
_____
_____
_____

Have you ever written them down before?

_____
_____
_____
_____
_____

THE GOAL TENDER

What would be the impact if you did write them down?

___

Write down 3–5 goals for this year.

___

ACTION PLANNER

ACTION PLANNER: CHAPTER TWO

Do you believe your goals are realistic? Why or why not?

_____
_____
_____
_____
_____

Do you believe your goals are achievable? Why or why not?

_____
_____
_____
_____
_____

In your mind, what beliefs do you need to **change** to achieve your goals?

_____
_____
_____
_____
_____

THE GOAL TENDER

Write down your goals from the **Chapter One Action Planner**. Now by each one, write down how you can make it specific and measurable.

Goal	Specific	Measurement

ACTION PLANNER

ACTION PLANNER: CHAPTER THREE

If you own a company, do you have a mission statement?

_____
_____
_____
_____
_____

If you don't have a company, what is your personal mission statement?

_____
_____
_____
_____
_____

If you don't have one, create one here:

_____
_____
_____
_____
_____

THE GOAL TENDER

What are your one-year goals?

_____
_____
_____
_____
_____

What are your two-year goals?

_____
_____
_____
_____
_____

What are your three-year goals?

_____
_____
_____
_____
_____

ACTION PLANNER: CHAPTER FOUR

Do you have a mission statement for your life and your work?

_____
_____
_____
_____
_____

Do you write down goals that could be bigger?

_____
_____
_____
_____
_____

What holds you back from setting bigger goals?

_____
_____
_____
_____
_____

THE GOAL TENDER

Do you believe in your dreams? Do you believe you deserve them? Do you believe they are possible?

_____
_____
_____
_____
_____

How can you deflect and block negative comments and limited thinking from other people?

_____
_____
_____
_____
_____

ACTION PLANNER

ACTION PLANNER: CHAPTER FIVE

Do you associate with any negative people (ESVs)? Who are they and why do you associate with them?

_____
_____
_____
_____
_____
_____
_____

Do you associate with positive people? Who are they? Who are some positive people you can have more interaction with?

_____
_____
_____
_____
_____
_____
_____

THE GOAL TENDER

Who can be your support team for your goals at work and at home?

_____
_____
_____
_____
_____

Write down one of your major goals here, and make a list of the key priorities.

_____
_____
_____
_____
_____

Do you write your goals and priorities down in your calendar (electronic or physical)?

_____
_____
_____
_____
_____

ACTION PLANNER

ACTION PLANNER: CHAPTER SIX

Have you made a list of all your EBCs? Who are they and how can you associate with them more?

_____
_____
_____
_____
_____

Have you created a master list of tasks for all your goals?

_____
_____
_____
_____
_____

Have you started using a weekly list? If not, when will you start?

_____
_____
_____
_____
_____

THE GOAL TENDER

Have you started writing a daily list? If not, when will you start?

_____
_____
_____
_____
_____

As far as thinking about your goals, what have you changed? What has been the impact?

_____
_____
_____
_____
_____

What thinking do you still need to work on or change?

_____
_____
_____
_____
_____

ACTION PLANNER: CHAPTER SEVEN

Have you ever studied the law of attraction? What book can you read to learn more about it?

_____
_____
_____
_____
_____

Can you see how it would be part of goal setting?

_____
_____
_____
_____
_____

On your list of goals, do you have a measurement for each goal? How do you think this would make a difference?

_____
_____
_____
_____
_____

THE GOAL TENDER

On your list of goals, do you have dates for completion by each one? How do you think this would make a difference?

_____
_____
_____
_____
_____

How do you think having measurements and dates will help you in terms of holding yourself accountable?

_____
_____
_____
_____
_____

What are other ways you can think about holding yourself accountable?

_____
_____
_____
_____
_____

ACTION PLANNER

ACTION PLANNER: CHAPTER EIGHT

Do you have time planned each day for morning reading? Do you think it could make a difference for you?

_____
_____
_____
_____

When you plan your morning reading, what are some topics you want to learn and read about?

_____
_____
_____
_____

What system or technology do you use to manage your appointments?

_____
_____
_____
_____

THE GOAL TENDER

What system or technology do you use to manage your goals?

_____

_____

_____

_____

_____

What other technology can you use to help with your goals?

_____

_____

_____

_____

_____

ACTION PLANNER

ACTION PLANNER: CHAPTER NINE

Are you aware of what you say to yourself every day? Are they negative or positive statements?

_____
_____
_____
_____

Do your ever deflect compliments or downplay big ideas? Why do you think that you do that?

_____
_____
_____
_____

Have you ever heard of a vision board? Would you consider creating one? What do you think the impact could be?

_____
_____
_____
_____
_____

THE GOAL TENDER

Have you ever tried spoken affirmations? Would you be willing to try them?

_____
_____
_____
_____
_____

Have you ever tried written affirmations? Would you be willing to try them?

_____
_____
_____
_____
_____

ABOUT SHAWN DOYLE CSP

Hi, I'm Shawn Doyle CSP. It's nice to meet you! I am a certified professional speaker with the CSP designation. I'm sure you have heard of board-certified surgeons—I am a board-certified speaker. Only 12 percent of speakers in the world have this designation, so I am very proud of that, and it is a mark of quality for you. I am also a certified corporate coach. My life passion is to make a positive difference in people's lives by helping them live to their full potential both at work and at home as people go through something called life.

I have spent almost three decades in the world of personal and professional development, and from 2000–2003, I cofounded a Corporate University for Comcast, where I was Vice President of Learning and Development. I have many amazing clients, some of which include Pfizer, Zippo,

Comcast, Lockheed Martin, NBC, Aberdeen Proving Grounds, Guidepost, ABC, Disney, Kraft, the US Marines, Charter, The Ladders, and IBM.

I am known for my thought-provoking, fun, and highly interactive training programs and keynotes. That means you will get the results you are looking for, and I guarantee it. The biggest compliment I get is being asked to come back again and again to work with my clients.

I am the author of 21 books, some of which include: *The Ten Foundations of Motivation, Sales Science, 6 Essentials of Success, Dr. Babb's Idea Lab, The Manager's Pocket Guide to Motivating Employees, The Managers Pocket Guide to Training, Juiced! How to be more creative in business and in life!, 2 Months to Motivation!, Jumpstart Your Motivation, The Soul Survivor, Jumpstart Your Leadership, Jumpstart Your Creativity, The Sun Still Rises, Jumpstart Your Customer Service, Jumpstart Your Business, Jumpstart Your Networking,* and *Jumpstart Your Productivity.* I am a contributing writer for *The Huffington Post, Inc., Entrepreneur, The Good Men Project,* and *Addicted2success.*

Four of my books are now being translated into ten languages and being distributed and sold in India, Malaysia,

Singapore, China, Canada, Russia, and Greece. I live in the rolling hills of southwestern Pennsylvania, made famous by Andrew Wythe landscape paintings. I share my life with an amazing, wonderful wife and three crazy cats. My website is www.shawndoylemotivates.com.

www.ingramcontent.com/pod-product-compliance
Lightning Source LLC
Chambersburg PA
CBHW070453100426
42743CB00010B/1599